MW01032607

Table of Contents

Chapter 1

Throw Out Traditional Marketing

Yes, you read the chapter title correctly. It's time to change the way you market your business. No more newspaper ads or budget-busting phone book advertising. No more coupon value packs where your ad is buried in the midst of your competitors. It's time to learn how to make your business stand out from your competition while not breaking the bank on costly marketing efforts that just don't work.

To be honest, you get kudos for the fact that you are doing any marketing at all. Many contractors don't have a marketing program simply because they don't know what to do or do not see the need. Those that are marketing their businesses aren't always doing it the right way, not for a lack of effort, but simply because it's not their area of expertise. Roofing contractors are experts in roofing, usually not marketing.

You may know that it's a good idea to engage in some kind of marketing for your business, but how do you know what you should be doing? When most people think of marketing, their minds immediately go to advertising and they end up buying some ads in local publications and phone books without really knowing if they are reaching their target audience. So while ads are definitely better than no marketing at all, there are ways to maximize your marketing efforts with specific, targeted activities that will deliver a much higher return on investment (ROI).

Do I even need to market my business?

There are probably some of you who are thinking "I'm busy enough right now and have jobs scheduled out for the next few months so why would I want to bring in more work?" Keep in mind that marketing your business is something that needs to be done on an ongoing basis. Why? Because it will sustain your business when you hit the times of year that may be a little lean or keep you afloat during a milder-than-normal weather year that results in little strain to the roofs in your market. A long-term, sustained marketing program can make the difference when it comes to staying profitable during economic downturns.

Ongoing marketing creates top-of-mind awareness which means that potential customers will think of your company when they have a need for your services. As you read through this book, you will learn how to do this in ways that are not cost prohibitive and can also deliver results.

Marketing is about more than just running an ad. It's about establishing your business as a member of the community and establishing your employees as friends and colleagues who live, work and attend church in the same community as your customers. Being a part of the community is critical to your success.

For any good marketing program, it is crucial that the first step be self-evaluation. To create or improve your marketing program you need to first analyze it. How does your current marketing work with your overall business practices? Review what you like and do not like about your current sales and marketing process. Create a leadership team who will help you evaluate sales and marketing and the business overall. The leadership team should be made up of key personnel in the company. This will be different for each company but usually would include the directors of finance, operations, marketing and sales. This team should focus on an overall evaluation that helps establish mission statements, goals and brand.

Don't stop there, ask your networks, ask your employees, ask your customers, and ask your friends, how your company is viewed in the community and what you might be able to do to increase your brand exposure. In Appendix 1 we provide a sample survey that may be the baseline you need for getting started.

Getting out of the marketing rut
So just how do you get out of the marketing rut? You are taking the first step by reading this book. As you explore the chapters you will learn

about how marketing is an integral part of the sales process. It plays a role in how you manage and handle your leads; how you generate leads and how you make your sales presentation. Marketing is prevalent throughout the job itself and after the job is complete. It's one of those things that is intertwined into your day-to-day activities and plays a larger role than you might think.

As you progress through this book, you'll have ample opportunity to evaluate your current business practices and develop a plan to guide you into a strong sales and marketing process. It's going to take a little bit of effort on the part of you and your leadership team but in the end you will have a direction, a plan, an idea of budget and you will understand how to implement your efforts for sustained success. Ready to get started?

Discussion topics for your leadership team

Is my business currently doing any marketing or advertising?

What parts of our business need marketing priority?

How much are we spending on marketing and advertising?

Is the current sales and marketing program working?

What should be changed?

Are we getting new customers?

What are the customers saying?

Do we understand the changing market demographics of our community?

Action items

Ask incoming callers how they heard of your company and keep an ongoing record.

Ask your employees what they think of your current marketing and how it is working.

Survey your employees concerning company communications.

If you are currently advertising locally, ask the media sources for demographic information and statistics on how your current advertising is working.

Chapter 2

Evaluating the Sales Process

The first step for any marketing program is determining need and following through. What does that mean? It means "Do you need leads?" And if you get them, "What are you going to do with them?" That may seem strange, since it should be obvious that all businesses need sales leads. But using an example from a roofing contractor in California who thought all would be fixed if he could just get leads, it does not always work that way. In sharing his story, it may seem familiar.

Joe's residential roofing business had been stagnant. Although Joe had great relationships in his community and within the roofing industry, he did not understand why the business was not growing. Reaching out, he met with a number of friends and industry experts. Following their advice, he sat with his leadership team and decided to evaluate his overall sales and marketing process.

His first step was to look at his sales team. Currently his sales team consisted of one full time sales person and himself. He figured that between running the company and selling he was half time. So he did some calculations. How many leads could he handle in a week and continue to provide the type of service that he believes in?

He also considered that not every phone call turns into a sales call. In fact, in reviewing his sales efforts at the front desk, his office manager was able to set appointments for about half of the calls. So he figured he would need at least twice the number of leads coming in over the phone. His team agreed that 42 leads per week would be a good number. (See Appendix 4 for example of a Lead Calculator)

Joe then looked at his leads. He had been using traditional marketing tools in the form of yellow page and radio ads. He had also recently engaged a marketing firm to help with digital marketing. He felt that he needed to get in front of more customers with articles and information.

The marketing firm was sending out weekly e-blasts utilizing his Customer Relationship Management (CRM) software. It seemed like he should be doing great; however, he had not been tracking how customers were finding out about him. The team determined that it was important to know where the leads were coming from and, with some honest discussion, they needed to determine how they were handling the leads. The other key discussion was, did they really know how many leads they were getting and what was happening to them?

The team went to work to determine numbers and origination of leads. It soon became clear that there were a number of leads coming in, in fact far more than the 42 leads they had targeted per week. The team realized that they needed to understand the quality of these leads and make sure their marketing was bringing in the right clientele. They developed a questionnaire that walked their leadership team through some important questions. (See Appendix 2 for sample lead questionnaire.) After reviewing the questions, the team took it one step further, evaluating and determining how they wanted the process to look for handling leads.

In the end, Joe's leadership team determined that what they really needed was an additional sales person and some revamping of their marketing to make sure the right customers were being targeted. They looked at the strengths of the company, the types of jobs that were profitable, rewarding and helped generate additional referrals. For Joe's Roofing that meant a strong emphasis on older neighborhoods with higher-end, more difficult roofing jobs. They started targeting these types of homes with articles on maintenance, preservation and ways of minimizing disruption. With a strong commitment to good customer relations, satisfaction and ongoing education, Joe's reputation continued to grow and the business supported additional hires in sales and sales support. All of which led to growing the business.

Every company is different. It is critical for companies to commit time to marketing strategy and evaluation every year with check-ins every quarter. We are going to talk more about employees as brand ambassadors but the beginning of strong marketing is a strong engagement of employees in the sales and marketing evaluation and process. All aspects of the company from production to finance to sales, influence the brand of a roofing company. Their participation in the overall strategy and commitment to the goals that are set will make the difference between a successful or unsuccessful marketing plan and subsequent sales and profitability. It starts at the top with you.

Discussion topics for your leadership team

What is your current sales lead process, beginning to end?

How many leads can the company handle a week to meet brand and quality standards?

Who is your audience and how do you make sure you are receiving leads from that audience?

How does the marketing program support the right leads and in turn sales?

Action items

Leadership team utilize lead calculator to evaluate need.

Leadership team to build chart tracking lead process through the sale and to referral.

Share results with sales and marketing team if they are not part of leadership and ask for feedback.

Chapter 3

Generating Leads

Now that you've evaluated your sales process and have that in shape the next step is generating leads. There isn't one easy answer on how to generate a lead nor is there one activity that works better than all others. It's a combination of activities that you and your team should be doing every day to cultivate relationships, build awareness and bring in the lead. There is preparation for gathering leads that goes beyond goals and processes and that is the logistics of how to gather and where to store leads. Before we dive into generating leads we need to talk about Customer Relationship Management (CRM) software.

Customer Relations Management

When generating leads there is an ongoing need to not only attract customers but sustain them over long periods of time. Whether it is homeowners or building owners, they need to be nurtured so that your company is top of mind when they have roofing needs or have the opportunity to refer your company.

So how can this happen? It starts with a strong CRM software. What is that? Well it could be Microsoft Outlook or an Excel file or on a higher level software such as Salesforce. In the roofing world, there are many contractor CRM software systems that help manage customers and often are connected to project management and/or accounting software.

Whichever CRM you use, the key is to maintain a strong, up-to-date list of customers. By using a CRM software instead of Excel or a Rolodex, customer contact can be automated. This will include notes, past correspondence, property data, material preferences and/or future projects.

Contact information including email addresses that are sitting in filing cabinets and not in an up-to-date CRM are useless. In fact, many contractors have hired summer interns to simply capture information that has been in project files. When they enter the information it is key to add as much data as possible. Information is critical in order to properly segment your customers and offer strong communications.

Once a CRM program is in place and information, past and present has been entered, you will have an organized way of capturing leads and utilizing them for long-term marketing. Following you will find several marketing strategies that can feed your overall customer list. As discussed in the chapter before, work with your leadership team to see which of these tools make sense. You do not need to incorporate them all at once but intertwine them in a strong overall marketing strategy that will drive sales and brand awareness.

Public Relations

Let's start with one activity that doesn't cost anything – public relations. You've probably heard of public relations or PR but what is it? Simply put, PR is the relationship between your business and its customers (or potential customers).

As we saw with Joe, he realized that communicating the strengths and knowledge of his company and team would make an impact on current and future customers.

So what does that mean? It means you want to position your business in your local community as a resource, as a company that provides information and shared expertise. You want to be top of mind for potential customers so when a need for your service arises, they will think of you.

Getting started with PR

Start small with news that is easy to share. Did you hire a new employee? Did someone get a promotion? Are you adding a new service program or division? What charitable activities is your company participating in? Tell the community about it through a press release to your local newspaper and business journal. Don't be intimidated by writing a press release, it's just the basic information or the who, what, when, where and why. Search on the internet for a sample press release to use as a guide or use our sample press release in Appendix 5 as a starting point.

The next step is to reach out to local media and position your company as the local expert. Newspapers, TV and radio stations all have news slots that they are looking to fill with content. Why not have it be your content? Seasonal changes and weather events are a great time to provide information to your local media. This is where you share your expertise. If you are advertising locally, this should be a given as part of your advertising contract.

Contractors have a great play when it comes to the seasons. For example, in the heart of fall, provide information on what homeowners should be doing to prepare their homes and roofs to protect them throughout the winter. A simple tip sheet of to-do's is an easy piece for the media to share with their viewers or readers. You already know what these should be –include tasks such as clearing leaves and debris from gutters, ensure downspouts are clear, engage a local roofing contractor (you) to perform a pre-winter inspection to address any issues that may exist. Throw in some tips about winter safety including some education on ice dams and safely clearing snow from the roof (call a contractor).

The same thing can be done in the springtime. As the winter begins to thaw, tell the community what homeowners should be doing to ensure their roof is still in good shape for the coming April showers. Just about all local media outlets have their reporters' contact numbers and email addresses available on their websites making it really easy to get in touch with them.

Local Organizations

Are you a member of the local Chamber of Commerce, Rotary Club, Jaycees or other organization? If so that's great, but do you attend their events and activities? People do business with people that they know. So get to know the other members in these groups. Most have monthly meetings or networking events that are the perfect platform to build strong relationships. Members will get to know you and when the time comes that they need a roofing contractor you can bet that you will be at the top of their mind. And better yet, if a friend or associate asks if they know a good contractor, you can be sure they will pass along your name.

You may be thinking that you just don't have time to join a local organization. Between, work, your family and your kids' school activities there isn't a lot of time left is there? If you can't commit to an organization, why not get involved with your children's school? Or maybe some of your employees are already members and they could attend for you. There are most likely other members of your team that support the booster club, or volunteer to work the snack stand on a weekend game. Consider buying a small ad in the sports program, it's not only good advertising but great public relations. All of this relationship building will result in leads for your business.

In-person Lead Gathering

While networking and relationship building within organizations is one way to generate leads, there's still many other homeowners in your service area who you may never meet through your community involvement. Right now they are strangers who may need your services but they aren't sure who to trust or who will do a reliable job for them. Let's take a look at a few ways to reach these potential customers.

Home Improvement Shows

Home improvement shows are generally attended by homeowners who will be taking action on a project such as a new roof in the very near future. They attend these shows to get ideas, see what's new, meet contractors and establish a dialogue regarding their needs.

Some contractors don't like participating in home shows because they perceive it as a negative to be positioned in the same building as many of their competitors. This is the wrong perception! This is your chance to stand out from your competitors and be the obvious choice for the attendees' next roof. If you are not there, then they are talking to your competition!

It sounds like a good plan, but just how does one stand out within a room full of competitors? Do what your competitors are not doing. There was a roofing company in the Midwest who did just that. They rented a space at their local home show and beyond the standard backdrop and manufacturer samples, they integrated technology into their booth. Technology that allowed the homeowner to receive an aerial view of their home and overall squares of the roof within the hour.

This contractor equipped his booth with a laptop, printer and tablet and while talking to a lead, would use his tablet to order the report and request that a copy be emailed to the prospect. This allowed him to gather critical CRM information including their name, address and email address. The potential customers were asked to come back in an hour to receive their printed copy.

Every single one of them came back to get the printout that contained the image and information along with the contractor's contact information. At that time the contractor scheduled an appointment for the home visit to deliver the full estimate. Not only did he now have a lead but he had critical overall contact information for his long-term marketing.

This was a great success for this contractor because he established the relationship at the show and was able to position himself as a forward-thinking business owner who used the latest technologies to ensure an accurate estimate and smooth job process.

Canvassing

Canvassing, also known as door knocking, has been around for years as a lead-gathering tool. Why? Because it works! You want to take care that you are doing it properly.

Outfit your canvassers with shirts displaying the company logo. Providing them with a photo ID badge to wear will instill confidence in homeowners that your company is a professional organization. Not every homeowner will be at home so it's important to have a piece of literature that you can leave at their door.

You may not always be able to schedule an appointment at the time you speak with a homeowner. They may need to consult a spouse or work schedule. Take down their information on an appointment form and tell them that since you respect their privacy, would they please sign at the bottom of the form to give you permission to call or email them. With do not call lists and anti-spam laws, it's important to document that you asked and received permission. It is even more important to gather strong marketing lists that have come from reliable sources.

Some may worry about the cost of canvassing. There are a couple of options. A contractor out of Oregon recruited college students to canvass during their summer break. It was a great opportunity for the college students to learn more about the trades and make a great income over the summer. Many contractors hire canvassers on commission only but this can be tricky. Commission-based sales, especially canvassing, can become pressure oriented which can hurt the company's brand. Be sure to hire canvassers who can sell but also maintain a great image for the company overall.

Homeowner Associations

Homeowner associations (HOAs) are often not thought of as a way to generate leads but can give you virtually exclusive access to an entire neighborhood. It's not always easy to find them or establish contact but once you do, this can be well worth the effort.

There was an HOA community of 190 duplex homes in the mid-Atlantic region. The insurance company for the community was requiring roof inspections due to the large number of leak claims surrounding aging pipe collars. The members of the HOA board reached out to a local roofing contractor that one of the board members knew through community involvement (remember earlier we mentioned the importance of networking) and the contractor was retained to inspect all of the homes.

The contractor took the opportunity to offer any homeowner that had to replace a pipe collar a discount for that same amount should they choose to replace their roof with his company. He is now listed on the community's website and in their newsletters as a resource for roofing needs. It has resulted in many jobs for his business.

So as you establish your community relationships and continue to network, ask those connections if they have an HOA or neighborhood association. Be sure to offer your services.

Discussion topics for your leadership team

How are we currently generating leads?

What are doing well and what could we be doing better?

Evaluate your team's strengths. Does someone stand out as a great in-person lead generator? Does someone else have strong organizational and/or writing skills? Is someone techy and into social media? Who is already involved in community organizations?

Action items

Identify what lead generating activities you want to do.

Assign members of your team as owners of that activity and schedule weekly touch-base meetings to monitor progress.

Chapter 4

Marketing for the New Age

Networking and in-person lead generation is great but there are newer and more cost-effective ways to keep your name in front of the community that you will need to consider. Top-of-mind awareness is key to producing leads later. Not every homeowner has a need for your service but when they do or have a friend who does, you want them to think of you first.

Reinventing traditional tools

Traditional tools can sometimes work in your favor when it comes to utilizing tools such as yard signs, truck magnets or door hangers. But why not take these traditional tools to the next level to really get your customers' attention?

Instead of using door hangers why not create a neighborhood notice that you can print out at a local office supply store or digital printer? A neighborhood notice is essentially a flyer that you can leave tucked in the doors of neighbors that are located near where you have a job in production. Include a message that lets them know you are currently working on their neighbor's roof and apologize in advance for any noise. Be sure to include an offer such as a discount on their job if they choose to contact you to bid on their roofing needs.

Free marketing support and services

As you are reading through these great ideas you may be thinking that it sounds like you might have to spend a lot of money to implement some of these initiatives. Not necessarily. While it's true that every successful company has to be willing to invest some dollars in marketing and lead generation (we'll cover this in the chapter on budgeting) there are ways to minimize out-of-pocket costs.

Don't forget about your manufacturers and suppliers. Many have cooperative advertising (coop) programs that will contribute dollars toward marketing initiatives that include their logo. There are different guidelines for what is covered and there might be paperwork involved but this is free marketing money! In many coop programs, contractors earn dollars based on material purchases or warranties sold. These same programs will often see those dollars expire at the end of the year if not used. Don't be one of the contractors that leaves thousands of dollars sitting on the table.

There are even manufacturers that will design and provide co-branded materials for you to use in presentations and marketing efforts. All you need to do is ask your sales representative and they can give you details of their particular program.

Using the web and social media

If there is one place to reach just about anyone these days, it's on social media and the Internet. Do you have a Facebook or Twitter account? More than one billion people have Facebook accounts and Twitter sees more than 243 million active users each month. It's critical for your business to have an online presence.

Don't have a social media presence? Worried about not knowing how to do it? It's worth the effort to learn (kids and grandkids are great teachers) but if you still are unsure consider hiring a summer college intern who can get your business on social media and train you or someone on your team to manage the social media. Studies have shown that the number of people trusting a friend's recommendation for a service or product comes in at about 90%, versus the number of people who trust an advertisement which comes in at only 14%. When your business has a presence on social media, you are becoming a trusted friend.

In addition to the wealth of personal social networking sites that are out there be sure you don't forget about LinkedIn. This is more of a business and professional networking site that allows you to take the in-person networking that you have done through your community involvement and extend it to the online realm.

Website and online leads

In the past, the Yellow Pages was the main resource consumers turned to when they wanted to locate a contractor or were looking for a specific service. That behavior has shifted as consumers rely on the World Wide Web to search for services in their area. In fact, if you asked someone born in the last 15 years what the Yellow Pages are, they probably are not going to know what you are talking about!

Your website is your new Yellow Pages ad. It needs to provide enough information about your company in such a way that potential customers will take action and request an estimate for their job. A customer wants to feel confident that you are experienced, that your team is professional, that you are backed or trained by leading manufacturers, that you will support your work with service afterward if needed and that you are knowledgeable about the latest products and technologies. Be sure to include customer testimonials with some before and after photos. They hold a lot of weight.

Your website should be dynamic, meaning that the content is fresh and always up to date. Have a section on your site that provides short articles and information that your customers will find interesting. Post your press releases and other news regularly on your site.

In addition to communicating the confidence-building information mentioned previously, you want to start a relationship. Help that potential customer see you the same way they see themselves – as a person with a family who works hard. Tell your story. How did your business start? Has it been in the family for generations? List your community involvement. Show pictures of your team so the customer humanizes your company.

A good website will have a prominent button or link on every page that a visitor can click on to request an estimate. Ask them to complete a form that captures their contact information (name, address, phone and email) but also use the opportunity to gather some basic qualifying information. This could be the age of their roof, the age of their home and what style roof they are interested in. Try to limit the questions to three or four and make them optional. You don't want to risk losing a lead because they were impatient with the form.

Since you already reviewed your processes in chapter one of this book, you should have the steps in place to follow up on the lead after the website form is submitted.

Implementing an e-mail program

As you capture customer information and email addresses, it's important to think about how you will communicate with them moving forward. Maintaining contact with your customers and potential customers is what keeps your company top of mind when a need arises.

Start out slowly by sending quarterly emails. Provide useful tips and information similar to the content that you provide each season to the local media. Consider profiling an employee of the quarter. Highlight any community involvement.

Look for subscription-based email programs, like Constant Contact®, that charge a monthly fee for services or charge based on the number of contacts and emails you send. This can be a very affordable way to stay in front of your customers.

Discussion topics for your leadership team

Which of these lead generating activities could you implement immediately with the resources we have today?

Are there resources nearby such as a local college with a marketing program that could work with you as a class project?

Does a current employee have experience with websites, email or social media?

What companies are in the industry who could be evaluated for services in this area?

Action items

Identify what lead generating activities you want to do.

Assign members of your team as owners of that activity and schedule weekly touch-base meetings to monitor progress.

Ask other contractors in your network or association for referrals.

Chapter 5

Turning the Lead into a Sale

You've done your work generating the lead and have scheduled the sales appointment. Now it's time to review what you can do to increase your chances of turning that lead into a sale.

Customer experience

It might seem obvious, but the better you can make the overall experience for the customer, the higher the likelihood that you will close the sale. The experience starts when the lead comes in and then continues through the sales call.

Follow the same general rules for your sales team that were discussed in the previous chapter regarding canvassers. Appearances matter. Supply your sales team with professional shirts bearing your company logo and ban jeans from sales calls. Be sure that vehicles are clean. A photo identification badge adds reassurance that your company is legitimate and safety conscious.

Secure and review aerial images of the property before the initial homeowner meeting. If there are any areas of concern, it's important to know about it ahead of time and not be caught off guard by a roof that presents special challenges. At the appointment, invite the owner to walk around the outside of the property with you. You can easily verify things that you may have noticed in the aerial images that you reviewed prior to the appointment and educate the homeowner at the same time. Use this opportunity to ask them if there are any concerns with children, pets or neighbors that your company should be aware of while the work is being done. This sends a subliminal message that your company is careful and considerate.

Be respectful of the customer's home. After the walk around and before entering the home, wipe your feet and if the weather is bad, carry a set of booties to slip over your shoes to avoid tracking dirt or mud into the home. This reinforces the careful and considerate message that you started sending during the outside walk around.

Professional presentation

Once inside the home the presentation should be concise, professional and interactive. Get the homeowners involved in the presentation. How? It's easy to do when you integrate technology into the meeting and it's not expensive to get started using it.

Your entire sales team should be armed with mobile tools such as an iPad® or Android™ powered tablet. As the technology has advanced, prices for these devices have dropped. The iPad or tablet should be a critical part of the entire presentation and we'll look at how to use it in the next few paragraphs.

Before pulling out the technology, start the presentation by helping the customer get to know you as a person. This is easily accomplished by sharing a few photos and interesting information. Do you coach your son's baseball team? Do you lead your daughter's Girl Scout troop? Volunteer with a nonprofit organization? We all know that people buy from people so starting off by finding common ground and building a relationship is the right first step.

Next the customer needs to get to know your company a little better. This is when you can use the tablet for a quick presentation about the company. Review the basics such as years in business, list of manufacturer certifications, some before and after photos of your work and a testimonial.

Now it's time to make the presentation be about the customer and their home. Review the aerial images of their home. Point out any areas where you may have noticed delicate landscaping and note that your production team will take extra precautions in those places to not damage flowers or shrubs. Show them where the materials will be staged or the dumpster positioned. This attention to detail is one more tie back to the fact that your company is meticulous and respectful of their property.

Use the mobile device to visit the manufacturer's website. At this point, make the presentation interactive. Hand over the tablet so the homeowners can browse the different styles and colors of shingles or tiles.

You'll be sure to really make an impact if you use your mobile device to snap a picture of the customer's home from the curb upon your arrival. After reviewing the styles and colors available, upload that photo to a visualizer website (if your manufacturer offers one) and hand the mobile device back to the homeowner so they can experiment with how different colors look on their home.

Customers want to be sure that you will be around after the job is complete to address any issues that may arise or just for routine service. Tell them about your maintenance division if you have one and review any manufacturer's warranty that comes with the roofing products they are interested in.

Close the sale

Every salesperson wants a one-trip close but sometimes that doesn't happen on the first appointment. This is why follow up is critical. The more touch points you can have with the customer, the higher the chance that you will get the sale.

Follow up is critical at this point. The customer's experience with their initial inquiry and the sales call sets the tone and their expectation of how the job will go if they choose to hire you. If there is no follow up after the initial meeting that might leave a bad image in the customer's mind of how the roof installation experience will be.

An email immediately following the presentation is a nice touch. Simply thank them for their time and mention something unique or interesting that was discussed during the visit that is related to the common ground you may have established. For example, if you both coach, maybe this would be an opportunity to share a link to a coaching website that is a good resource. The links to the manufacturer's website and to the visualizer tool can be included in the email as well as a copy of the image that was taken of the home from the curb. Emailing right away shows responsiveness and provides one more chance to strengthen the relationship.

Although some of this may seem very basic, many roofing professionals do not incorporate these techniques. In the end, the sales call is a reflection of the company's brand. If the sales call does not mirror marketing and production then it will cause confusion, even if only on a subliminal level, with the customer. When branding is consistent throughout the customer experience, it develops a deep sense of trust and loyalty.

Discussion topics for your leadership team

Evaluate your customers' experience. What are you doing right? What could you be doing better?

How are you using technology in your sales presentation?

Do you have a standard presentation style and process that you ask each salesperson to follow? Does it mirror marketing efforts and branding?

What is the follow-up process for after the sales appointment? Is there anything you could be doing differently?

Action items

Order team uniforms (shirts with logo, ID badges).

Purchase tablets or iPads.

Schedule training to learn how to use the devices to present.

Research what your manufacturers offer as far as visualization tools and style selectors.

Compare collateral and messaging throughout the entire customer experience to be sure it is consistent.

Chapter 6

After the Sale

Now that the job has been sold and the installation is complete, it's important to maintain an ongoing relationship with the customer.

Long-term relationships

You might be thinking that since the homeowner just put a new roof on their home, they aren't going to need another one for 20 years or more so why would you keep the relationship? Because maintaining a relationship will lead to more business – from the homeowner and from their friends, family and colleagues.

As mentioned in an earlier chapter, people trust recommendations from friends and family. In fact, a 2013 Nielsen Trust in Advertising survey found that word-of-mouth recommendations are the most influential with 84 percent of respondents across 58 countries indicating this was the most trusted source. By staying in contact with that homeowner your company remains top of mind. When a friend or family member in need of roof repair or replacement asks them about their experience or who they would recommend, your company will be the first one to be mentioned.

How should you stay in touch with a customer after a job is completed? There are many ways to accomplish this but perhaps the easiest is to add them to your seasonal or quarterly email recipient list. Use the content that you developed as part of your PR initiative that was discussed earlier in this book and send an email two to four times a year. Offer seasonal tips and information on the care and maintenance of their roof. Throw some non-roof related topics in there as well such as spring cleaning shortcuts or feature an employee's favorite recipe.

Don't forget that every customer touch point is an opportunity to sell. Use the regular emails as a vehicle to offer referral bonuses to former customers. When you sell a job to someone they refer, give the referral source a $50 Visa card and offer the new customer a $50 discount.

Maintenance Programs

The regular emails are also a great way to sell maintenance programs. As you educate the homeowners or business owner about the importance of roof maintenance, whether cleaning gutters or prepping roofs for the changing seasons, be sure to let them know that you offer a maintenance program and can easily complete these tasks for them. Consider adding an offer such as a discount if they mention that they learned about the program in the newsletter.

In addition to these informational emails that you send a few times a year do a special one for the various holidays. Send a happy Fourth of July email and share some fireworks safety tips – it' important to keep backyard fireworks far away from the roof! In the months before Christmas, why not pick a handful of customers each week that you can send an email to and let them know the measurements across their home or storefront roofline in order to make buying Christmas lights easier for them? They'll appreciate the personal touch and they will tell people about it, creating word-of-mouth buzz for your company. This is a great topic to pitch to the local newspapers or TV stations.

Testimonials

Don't forget about asking your customers to provide a testimonial after their job is completed. The easiest way is to send the customer a thank you email after the job is complete. Include a link to a simple feedback page that asks no more than five questions and provides a space for a free-form answer. You might want to ask questions such as:

- How satisfied were you with the installation of your new roof?
- Was the installation team professional and courteous?
- Did our team clean up the site to your satisfaction?

- How likely would you be to recommend our company to a friend or relative?
- Please tell us in your own words about your overall experience

Be sure to include a box that is checked by default that indicates "I give permission for the use of my comments on your website or in social media." Once you capture a testimonial be sure to use it!

Keep in mind that not every review will be positive. Negative feedback will give you an opportunity to address any issues within your team and also to re-establish a good relationship with an unhappy homeowner.

Social Media

It's time to share your excellent performance and work with the rest of the world! Take before and after photos of customers' homes. Be sure to include a statement in your service contract where the homeowner grants permission for you to publish before and after photos of their home. If they completed your feedback form and included a positive statement, this is a great thing to post along with the before and after photos to showcase your great work.

Discussion topics for your leadership team

What are you doing now as a company to maintain relationships?

How can you improve on what you are doing?

If you don't have a program, what are the resources it would take to start one?

If you have a maintenance program how are you marketing it to current and former customers?

Are you asking customers for testimonials?

What are you doing with the testimonials that you have?

Action Items

Establish an ongoing method for communications with customers for long-term relationships.

Develop a process for tracking and managing referral rewards (i.e. gift cards).

Create a process to collect customer testimonials through an email – online form method.

Sources: http://www.nielsen.com/us/en/newswire/2013/under-the-influence-consumer-trust-in-advertising.html

Chapter 7

Resources

Now that you understand how to generate a lead, what to do with the lead after you get it and how to maintain the relationship after the sale let's take a look at what resources are available to help you accomplish all of these goals. This chapter will explore technology, networking groups, continuing education, marketing budgets and how to coordinate all of these efforts.

Technology

Technology can be your friend and should be an important part of your business processes. It can seem intimidating at first but keep in mind that technology has progressed to the point that it's very intuitive and user friendly. It can help with organization, maintaining records of your customers and jobs and improve overall processes within your company. It's important for customers to see that you are a company that understands and utilizes technology in your operation. They will have more confidence in the contractor who presents a professional estimate, has an organized production schedule and can quickly and easily communicate before, during and after their job.

Hopefully you have your office equipped with computers and basic word processing and spreadsheet software as well as Internet access. A good, high-speed internet connection is important as much of today's estimating and customer relationship management (CRM) programs are web-based. Using a web-based CRM or estimating platform offer benefits in that you don't have to worry about storage or backup of your files.

There are platforms available that have been designed and built specifically for roofing contractors. Some are very robust and others are very basic. Many will offer a free 30-day trial so you can see if it has the features and functionality that meet your business needs.

Choosing from the many options can be difficult and seem overwhelming at times but it doesn't have to be. Start by reaching out to your roofing contractor association. Many vendors are associate members of the association and will participate in the annual conferences and trade shows. Find out when the trade show is and make a point to attend. It's a great way to visit with several vendors in one location and talk in person about what their software does and how it might fit with your business objectives. Most will offer specials at the shows and many are willing to send a trainer to your location to provide training and setup.

Be sure to ask the right questions. You'll want to know:

1. Are there annual licensing fees?
2. How many users at a time can be on the system?
3. What is their process for storage and backup of data?
4. Does the program integrate with other technology you may be using, such as aerial measurement reports?
5. If you decide to terminate using the program are there cancellation fees and who owns the data?
6. Is customer support available seven days a week?
7. Is onsite training available?

Networking Groups and Associations

An earlier chapter discussed how networking and participation in associations or organizations is critical for generating leads. The right groups can provide much more than leads for your business, they provide resources. If you aren't already a member of your local, regional and/or national roofing contractor associations you need to join today.

After joining, you need to familiarize yourself with what your association offers and take advantage of it. Most associations offer training, human resources support, access to discounted insurance, codes experts and financing services not only for your business needs but for you to offer to customers for their roof replacement or repair. Many will provide flyers and informative articles that you can use in your marketing efforts. You'll also be able to promote the fact that you are a member which instills confidence in customers. Be sure to ask if any vendors offer discount programs for association members; you can potentially save hundreds or thousands of dollars a year.

Beyond just taking advantage of your association's services and annual convention, ask if there are regular quarterly meetings that you can attend or if there are committees that you (or someone from your company) can serve on. It takes a minimal amount of time and allows you to build relationships with other roofing contractors in your state or around the country. Whether you've got a question or problem with a job, or if you are wondering what the best estimating software is for your business, you've established a network of resources that are just a phone call away.

Get started by contacting the National Roofing Contractors Association (NRCA) or visit their website at www.nrca.net. Look into membership and you will find a tremendous amount of resources available for you and your company. Through the national association you can also connect you with your local and regional associations.

Continuing Education

One of the most important things you can do for your business success is to take advantage of continuing education opportunities offered by the associations and vendors in the industry. Some states require a minimum number of hours of continuing education in different areas to maintain a license in good standing. Many trainings and classes are offered free of charge, often in conjunction with the annual conventions. There are also many opportunities to take advantage of online education. Online classes are ideal for days when the weather is not conducive to roofing.

In addition to maintaining compliance with state requirements, education allows you to stay on top of what is new in the industry. It also provides a public relations opportunity. After you or anyone on your team completes required hours, earns a certification or trains on new techniques, send a press release to your local newspaper and business journal. It's one more way to get your name out into the community to ensure you are remaining top of mind among customers. It also sends the subliminal message that your company cares about compliance and staying on top of the latest trends and technologies in the industry.

Budgeting

You probably know that you need to budget money for marketing but how much? The average amount that a business should allocate for ongoing, routine marketing is about three percent of gross revenue. That's just for normal marketing. If your company is trying to break into a new market area or focus on growing a particular service, the average is about eight to 10 percent.

The next question is how to allocate your funds. Categories should include:

- Printing and collateral production (for truck magnets, door hangers, etc.)
- Memberships (associations and civic groups)
- Home shows (exhibit space and graphics production)
- Subscriptions (email software, services)
- Freelancers (website creation/maintenance, graphic design, writing)
- Technology costs (website, social media, CRM)

It's not as simple as just splitting your budget evenly across the categories. The two categories that will take more resources are printing and collateral production or freelancers. You may be thinking that you have a website built already so why would you budget ongoing money for a freelancer to maintain it? As discussed earlier in the book, your website needs to be fluid and constantly evolving and growing. Don't forget about contacting your manufacturers for marketing assistance. Many offer coop funds that will help defray advertising costs and others will have materials ready where you can just add your logo.

You may want to consider hiring a consultant to come in and work with you to establish a marketing plan and budget for your business. Once you have it in place it can be managed by a marketing coordinator. This is an ideal position for a recent college graduate or someone with just a few years' experience. This person could also potentially update the website with a little bit of training or they may already have some website skills. With the right person in place, some of the money budgeted for freelance could possibly be redirected into salary for a full- or part-time position. If there are any colleges or universities nearby, you may be able to utilize an intern a few hours a week to help with your marketing efforts.

Discussion topics for your leadership team

What technology do we have in place now and is it meeting our needs?

Is there someone in our company who is particularly tech-savvy who could take the lead on this project?

What associations or groups is our company a member of and are we utilizing the resources of the group?

Do we have a formal training or education program in place? If not, what would it take to start?

How much are we spending on marketing every year? Is there a budget? How are we evaluating the success of what we are doing?

Action items

Evaluate current technologies such as estimating platforms and CRMs.

Create a list of associations to join and evaluate resources offered.

Establish formal training/education guidelines for your company.

Create a marketing plan and budget.

Contact distribution and manufacturers for marketing support.

Chapter 8

Your Brand and its Ambassadors

This chapter will discuss what a brand is and what it means for your business. Your brand is more than just a logo. It's your company's promise to its customers, it's the personality of your business and it can be a differentiating factor for you.

Brand Promise

A brand promise is what your company promises to deliver to its customers. So just what does your company deliver? You might say excellent service, quality roof installations and friendly staff. Those are all great things to deliver to your customer, but take time to dig a little deeper and really come up with what your company can promise the customer that not every other roofing company offers.

It's a good idea to conduct a brand audit. This doesn't have to be long and drawn out but find out what's important to your customers. Spend some time with your leadership team and discuss what customers say is most important to them. Have your sales team ask homeowners what their concerns are with the job. Take a look at other contractors in your area and what they promise customers.

To help you understand a brand promise and what it means for your business, we'll take a look throughout this chapter at a fictitious company that we'll call ABC Roofing. ABC Roofing's brand promise is: "ABC Roofing promises to provide a professional, quality installation safely, on time, with as little disruption as possible and we stand behind the installation."

Remember that a brand promise is serious. When you make a promise to your customer they develop expectations surrounding that promise. If you fail to deliver, customers will be let down, become confused and will begin to seek satisfaction elsewhere, from another brand.

Integrate your Brand

Your brand should be evident in everything you do, right down to how your staff answers the phone. Employees are your brand ambassadors and it's important for them to understand and agree with the brand promise. Let's examine how to integrate a brand promise into a business. If you recall, our fictitious company, ABC Roofing, developed a brand promise of:

"ABC Roofing promises to provide a professional, quality installation safely, on time, with as little disruption as possible and we stand behind the installation."

The first promise is to be professional. ABC Roofing has defined professional to mean:

- employees wear logo'd apparel and have ID badges
- trucks and vehicles are clean inside and out and bear the company logo
- no smoking on the jobsite
- booties are placed over shoes before entering customers' homes

The second part of the promise is to deliver a "quality installation, safely and on time." This is defined as:

- Being certified to install various manufacturers' products and system
- Taking advantage of ongoing training and learning opportunities
- Always adhering to OSHA rules and standards without cutting corners
- Showing up to start the job when promised

"With as little disruption as possible" is the next promise. ABC Roofing delivers on this by reviewing aerial photos of the home with the homeowner to determine the best areas for material delivery, dumpster positioning, access points and delicate landscaping to avoid. The company also asks questions about what to be aware of, such as if there are children that will be arriving home from school in the middle of the day.

Lastly, ABC Roofing has promised to "stand behind the installation." Most contractors will say they stand behind their installation but ABC Roofing goes a step further and provides a six month and one-year inspection at no cost to the customer. Not only does this send a strong message to the homeowner, it allows the company to have continued contact with them and provides an opportunity to sell an ongoing inspection and maintenance program at the end of the first year.

Brand Ambassadors

Simply put, your brand ambassadors are your employees. They represent your brand every day in the community. It's very important to have an onboarding process for new employees that includes training on your brand and its promise. If you and your team don't fully believe in the brand, your company will fail. Using the example of ABC Roofing, every employee should understand the brand promises and be able to not only repeat them but reflect them in everything they do.

Your employees are active in the community every day. They can be your best or worst sales representatives. If they are well versed and informed in what is going on in the company, they will not only talk about the company they work for but they will create a sense of trust and anticipation in their friends to work with and support your company.

By supporting your employees' involvement in community groups and activities, whether coaching a kids' team, or fundraising for the local Rotary, Kiwanis or Jaycees it's important that as an employer you offer the flexibility for employees to participate. It's a great extension of your brand and as mentioned in a previous chapter, networking generates leads and sales.

Discussion topics for your leadership team

Does our company have a brand promise? What is it?

Are we living our brand in our actions each day?

What is our employees' community involvement and how do we support it?

Action items

List out the elements that your brand promises to deliver.

Define exactly what those elements mean to the customer.

Determine how to educate employees on the brand promise.

Commit every day to communicating goals, marketing and messaging of your company with your employees to empower them as your brand ambassadors.

Appendix 1 – Company Sales and Marketing Questionnaire

The company sales and marketing questionnaire can be used during the evaluation stage. It will provide a baseline for evaluating the depth of understanding of your employees concerning your company brand and marketing strategy. By using this type of survey yearly, the leadership team can not only understand where the company is right now but also how it is improving year-over-year.

1. What is the mission of our company?

2. What are the goals and objectives of our company?

3. What are the key features and benefits of our services to our customers?

4. What are the marketing messages you are hearing from the company? (ads, blog, etc.)

5. How does your work support the company's goals and objectives?

6. Do you have access to the information you need to do your job in a way that supports the company's mission?

7. Do you feel that you are made aware of major changes that could affect your job or company direction?

8. Do you feel that employee opinions and suggestions are given significant consideration?

9. Do you see strong and consistent communication between the different departments?

10. If you were to share information on the company with a neighbor or friend, what would you say?

11. Would you recommend working here to a friend or family member?

Survey suggestions

1. First have your leadership team complete the survey. See how the leadership team does, which could lead to making adjustments before sharing with all employees.

2. Incentivize your employees to take their time and really think about the answers, it is important.

3. If necessary, make sure the survey is available in the language of your employees.

4. Do not be offended if the initial results are not stellar. It is a baseline for where you are going.

5. Work through the results with your leadership team and start making changes if needed.

6. Work with the sales and marketing team to create consistent messaging.

7. Create a similar survey for your customers after you feel you have made a cultural shift with employees to see how you are doing from an external perspective.

Appendix 2 – Lead Questionnaire

1. Where do we get our leads?
   a. Phone (How did they hear about us?)
   b. Web (How did they find us?)
   c. Cold Calls (How are you getting names?)
   d. Canvassing (How do we decide on neighborhood?)
   e. Events (home shows, county fair, open houses)
2. How do people hear about our company?
   a. Referrals
   b. Employees
   c. Advertising
   d. PR
   e. Social media
   f. Web search
   g. 3rd party lead generation
3. How do we treat leads?
   a. Timeframe for response
   b. Follow-up
   c. Qualifying
   d. Setting appointments
   e. Speed to estimate
   f. Follow up after the job
4. Who touches the leads?
   a. Inside sales representative (receptionist)
   b. Sales representative
   c. Estimator
   d. Production team – Supervisor
   e. Sales representative
5. How do we follow up after the close?
6. How do we follow up after the job?

Appendix 3 – Life of a Lead

1. Customer needs a roof

2. Talks to friends or business associates, does online research

3. Potential customer (lead) calls or emails Joe's Roofing

4. Appointed inside person returns call or email immediately and asks qualifying questions. (This may also be a fun form on the website that helps qualify).

5. Determines the needs and concerns of the customer and sets appointment

6. Salesperson calls lead to say thank you for the appointment, confirm participation and possibly do additional qualifying. (Does not always need to be the husband and wife, be respectful of the customer's time)

7. Salesperson then can prepare (or have inside person help prepare) introductory information and potential sales information using the qualifying questions, information and initial photos to make it personal and easy for the customer.

8. Initial sales call consists of building the relationship, inspecting the property and being prepared with the right information to take as little time as needed to move the customer to close.

9. Once closed, continue communications, set expectations and make it an easy and great experience.

10. Salesperson visits the job during production to make sure all is going well.

11. Supervisor builds relationship with customer through production to make sure they are happy.

12. With approval of customer, lawn signs, neighborhood notification flyers, door hangers or even special events are arranged to keep neighbors in the know about the project.

13. At the end of the job, the salesperson visits again with thank you packet that could include before-and-after photos, aerial imagery and measurement report, warranty materials and referral information for them to refer your company. At this time, they should ask to take a photo of the customers with their new roof for social media and as an overall thank you from Joe's Roofing for their business. It is also the perfect time to ask for referrals, testimonials, reviews or social media posts.

14. Joe personally sends thank you note after the job is complete with final photo of the new roof and a reminder of referral offers.

Appendix 4 – Lead Calculator

APPENDIX 4 - LEAD CALCULATOR

LEAD EVALUATION

Number of jobs desired per week	5
Sales closing rate	30%
Appointments to sales team per week	17
Appointment setting closing rate	50%
Number of leads needed per week	33

SALES EVALUATION

Number of appointments per salesperson per week (3 per day)	15
Number of appointments needed per week	17
Number of sales people needed	1.1

APPOINTMENT EVALUATION

Number of inbound & outbound calls per week (8 per day)	40
Number of appointments needed per week	33
Number of appointment setters needed	0.8

Appendix 5 – Sample Press Release

For Immediate Release
For More Information: _____
Phone: _____
Email: _____

ABC Roofing Company is Proud to Introduce New Employee

(City, State, Date) – ABC Roofing Company, the leading provider of roofing services for the greater Metro area, is pleased to announce the addition of Joe Smith as a lead estimator. He joins ABC Roofing Company in the important role of estimating and specializes in providing leading information on high quality and dependable roofing materials and services for both residential and commercial customers.

Smith brings strong roofing experience to the position. He began roofing during summer breaks, graduating from Mountain University in 2006. He has worked in all aspects of construction management with a focus on roofing systems and design. As an estimator for ABC Roofing, Smith will provide progressive design for roofing longevity and protection while focusing on value for both home and business owners.

ABC Roofing provides commercial roofing services that focus on quality craftsmanship, proven roofing materials and excellence in system engineering. "Joe Smith has been active within our community his entire career and understands the needs of our customers," stated John Brown, president of ABC Roofing. "We believe in this community and want to constantly provide the highest quality service for our customers. The roof is the ultimate protection of any building and we pride ourselves on taking care of our customers and community."

About ABC Roofing Company
Founded in 1965, ABC Roofing has been serving both the residential and commercial roofing needs of the metro area for 50 years. Committed to extraordinary craftsmanship, roofing system technology and exceptional customer service, ABC Roofing is proud to be a member of the Metro Chamber of Commerce and Better Business Bureau.

Appendix 6 – Sample Marketing Plan

Market Summary
- o Services Definition
  - ▪ Describe your services being marketed
- o Review changes in the market, which can include:
  - ▪ Market share
  - ▪ Leadership
  - ▪ Players
- o Competitive Landscape - Provide an overview of competitors
  - ▪ Competitors' strengths
  - ▪ Competitors' weaknesses
  - ▪ Services comparison and positioning
  - ▪ Pricing and costs

Positioning of Product or Service
- o Distinctly define your services features and benefits in the market and how they line up against competition
- o Define your value proposition
- o What is your Brand Promise?
- o Summarize the benefits of using your service to the consumer

Communication Strategies
- o List marketing messages for different audiences (commercial vs. residential, etc.)
- o List the demographics or profile of the targeted consumer groups

Public Relations Strategy and Execution
- o PR strategies and ideas, community engagement, new hires, product information, case studies, seasonal advice
- o PR plan including local media calendars, association engagements, home shows, case studies
- o Trade publication PR plan including case studies, awards, personnel profiles

Advertising Strategy and Execution
- o Overview of strategy, where are my customers and what are they engaged in
- o Overview of media and timing, seasonal opportunities, ongoing, new avenue
- o Overview of ad spending

Direct Marketing
- o Overview of strategy, vehicles, and timing, direct mailings, truck wraps, lawn signs
- o Overview of response targets, goals, and budget

Digital Marketing
- o Overview of strategy, e-mail, social media, website
- o Goals for lead generation

Third-Party Marketing
- o Describe co-marketing arrangements with distribution, manufacturing and technology

Appendix 7 – Sample Marketing Budget for Midsize Contractor

APPENDIX 7 – SAMPLE MARKETING BUDGET FOR MIDSIZE CONTRACTOR

Category	Estimated Quantity	Estimated Cost per Unit	Estimated Subtotal
OUTSOURCING			
Marketing consulting	2	$2,300.00	$4,600.00
Website support	1	$2,500.00	$2,500.00
SEO Optimization	12	$299.00	$3,588.00
Graphic design	60	$55.00	$3,300.00
Social Media Freelancer	12	$250.00	$6,000.00
Research Costs Total			**$19,988.00**
NETWORKING			
Association memberships	3	$100.00	$300.00
Affiliations	2	$20.00	$40.00
Subscriptions	2	$32.00	$64.00
Networking Costs Total			**$404.00**
PROMOTIONS			
Giveaways	50	$8.00	$400.00
Company clothing	200	$8.00	$1,600.00
Holiday gifts	200	$2.50	$500.00
Promotions Costs Total			**$2,500.00**
PRINTING			
Sales flyers (development & production)	5,000	$0.30	$1,500.00
Mailings/postcards (where is postage?)	15,000	$0.10	$1,500.00
Business Cards - All Employees	50	$25.00	$1,250.00
Promotions Costs Total			**$4,250.00**
ADVERTISING			
Google Ad Words	12	$250.00	$3,000.00
Television	2	$1,000.00	$2,000.00
Radio	4	$300.00	$1,200.00
Newspapers/Business Journal	6	$400.00	$2,400.00
Billboards	2	$1,000.00	$2,000.00
Bus sides	3	$125.00	$375.00
Advertising Costs Total			**$10,975.00**
PUBLIC RELATIONS			
Charity events	3	$200.00	$600.00
Program ads	4	$200.00	$800.00
Employee promotions	6	$200.00	$1,200.00
Sponsorships	3	$200.00	$600.00
Public Relations Costs Total			**$3,200.00**
ESTIMATED MARKETING GRAND TOTAL			**$41,317.00**

Appendix 8 – Sample Digital Marketing Plan

PLAN

- ✔ Create a digital marketing strategy
- ✔ Who is your audience?
- ✔ What do they need?
- ✔ How can you educate to create interest?

ATTRACT

- ✔ Grow your audience online
- ✔ Strong content
- ✔ Education
- ✔ Blog
- ✔ Search Engine Optimization (SEO)
- ✔ Keywords
- ✔ Social media

IMPLEMENT

- ✔ Encourage brand interactions and leads
- ✔ Forms
- ✔ Calls-to-actions
- ✔ Promotions
- ✔ Landing pages
- ✔ Give-a-ways
- ✔ Contests

CLOSE

- ✔ Increase sales communication
- ✔ Email
- ✔ Recognize buying signals and react
- ✔ Create opportunity
- ✔ Develop workflow
- ✔ Deliver leads

DELIGHT

- ✔ Build customer loyalty and advocacy
- ✔ Events
- ✔ Social
- ✔ Smart content
- ✔ Education
- ✔ Charity
- ✔ Community service

Conclusion

Thank you for taking the time to work through this introductory book on sales and marketing for roofing contractors. There is much more to learn but hopefully this has given you and your team a good start in evaluating, developing and improving sales and marketing for your company.

To continue the journey please visit our website at www.bizhak.com. We will be sharing articles, upcoming events and potential follow-up books in the future.

Credits

It has been an amazing experience working on this. The opportunity for us to collaborate on this has been incredible. We would like to thank all of the great contractors and marketers in the roofing business who we have had the pleasure of working with for many years.

Special thanks to the National Roofing Contractors Association and RoofersCoffeeShop.com for their support of this book, articles, webinars and speaking engagements.

Thank you to Paul Holzer for graphic support and interpretation. Also, we very much appreciate the help of the people who proofed this book not only for grammar but for concept and common sense. Thank you Vickie Sharples, Tim Ellsworth, Mike Duggan and Alison LaValley.

Finally, we would like to thank our families for their incredible support of this project. We could not do any of this without them!

Made in the USA
Middletown, DE
05 January 2022

57905191R00033